Bags of Gratitude

Kim Stanbrook

Gratitude
Kim Stanbrook

Design © 131 Design Ltd
www.131design.org
Images © Raphilena Bonito

Published 2016 by Tricorn Books
131 High Street, Old Portsmouth,
PO1 2HW

www.tricornbooks.co.uk

Printed & bound in UK

Bags of Gratitude

I dedicate this book to my parents, boyfriend, family and friends, for their love and support over the years for which I am filled with gratitude.

I dedicate this book to you, as you read the words and engage in thoughts of gratitude – thank you for joining me here.

Contents

Introduction   11

1 ❀ My Dream of Gratitude   13

2 ❀ The Cloak of Gratitude   15

3 ❀ Celebrate Each Day with Gratitude   17

4 ❀ Walking the Road of Gratitude   19

5 ❀ Messages of Gratitude   21

6 ❀ Gratitude is Here in the Moment   23

7 ❀ Radio Gratitude   25

8 ❀ Paint Your Picture of Gratitude   27

9 ❀ Who Are You, Gratitude?   29

10 ❀ Miracle of Gratitude   31

11 ❀ The Spirit of Gratitude   33

12 ❀ Knocking at the Door of Gratitude   35

13 ❀ The Dance of Gratitude   38

14 ❀ Fill Up Your Mind with Gratitude   40

15 ❀ Living a Life of Gratitude   42

16 ❀ Remember Gratitude?   43

17 ❀ The Gratitude Experience   45

18 ❧ The Light of Gratitude Shines Brightly   46

19 ❧ The Riches of Gratitude   48

20 ❧ Gratitude Unlocks Aspects of our Life   50

21 ❧ Awake to Gratitude   51

22 ❧ Gratitude for Happiness   53

23 ❧ Gratitude Comes Around   54

24 ❧ Call Me Gratitude   56

25 ❧ The Magic of Christmas – *I am Filled with Gratitude*   57

26 ❧ Special Dates of Gratitude   59

27 ❧ Gratitude – *The Legacy We Leave Behind Us*   62

28 ❧ Why Do I Love You, Gratitude?   64

29 ❧ Notes of Gratitude   66

30 ❧ Opening the Door to Gratitude   68

31 ❧ Joy of Gratitude   70

32 ❧ Gratitude Is The Secret!   72

33 ❧ Gratitude for Living   74

34 ❧ Gratitude – *Be Thankful Today*   76

35 ❧ Cultivate Gratitude   78

36 ❧ Flowers of Gratitude   80

37 ❧ Poems of Gratitude   81

38 ❧ Gratitude for Moments of Solitude   86

Final Thoughts   87

Bags of Gratitude

Introduction

Gratitude has always played a part in my life. Perhaps in the early years I didn't fully understand it all, but as I grew up I learned more about it. As a child I was taught to say 'thank you' to people for their gifts and to write a letter or a card. I have taken this habit with me into my adult life. Sometimes it has not been a letter but a phone call – it depends on the person.

I have also tried out a 'gratitude challenge' through an online card and gift service and this has helped me to be timely in my thanks and created an opportunity for me to be creative in what I send out.

There are lots of books on the subject of gratitude and I have dipped into many of them to learn more about the topic and what it means to other people.

A few years ago I decided to take part in a blogging challenge, which involved writing something about my chosen interest or topic each day for 30 days. This process helped to trigger ideas and as I worked through the challenge, I began to realise I enjoyed writing from the heart and being creative.

The chapters that follow were born from this blogging challenge and the ideas that flowed over the following months and years.

1

My Dream of Gratitude

It all started with a vivid dream one night where I found myself walking into a large store. It felt different, special, intriguing. In front of me, in fact all around me, were beautiful coloured bags – the ones made of strong card, with the stand-up handles made of rope. You know the ones?

They were all brightly coloured, all the colours of the rainbow and beyond – some sparkled, some were matt, some shiny, some striped, some covered with stars and some with pictures on the front.

"Where am I?" I asked.

The answer came back: "You are in the Bags of Gratitude."

"What is it?" I asked.

"This is the place where all the thoughts of gratitude are stored."

"Can I look around?"

"Of course. Be aware each bag belongs to someone, so take care as you look."

I didn't know where to begin, but the twinkling of the many bags drew me towards them. As I peered inside I could see many stars moving about, shining brightly. The messages I could hear, if I listened intently, told me that that person was radiating gratitude lots of times each day.

The warmth and power filled me for an instant – WOW!

A particular blue sparkly bag called to me and there I could see someone who wrote a gratitude journal each day, filled with their blessings.

It seemed, as I wandered about between the bags, depending on the resonance from them, that gratitude acts were either often or few.

The darkest of the bags, which I found at the edge, felt sad. Although it was shiny black on the outside, the thoughts I picked up were of someone who had lost sight of being grateful for their blessings and no longer connected to that energy and flow. They were somehow stuck.

I asked – "How can I help?"

The answer came: "Put into the bag a thought of gratitude"… and as I did so, a star broke out and shed some light – a shift occurred and the energy became lighter. I could hear someone remembering something special and the bag gleamed more.

"Sprinkle more thoughts of gratitude please," came back a message – so I did. The bag lightened to a pale blue. Then my alarm went off and I woke up! I remembered the dream straight away and was already thinking of what I was grateful for.

So make your bag of gratitude sparkle today – send out thoughts of gratitude. These thoughts will help make your bag resonate with positive energy and also help others who may need it.

Action: Imagine your bag of gratitude – what colour is it? How does it look? How does it feel? Now add in some thoughts of gratitude each day.

2

The Cloak of Gratitude

Each morning as we get up let's put around us our cloak of gratitude – it will keep us warm through the day and cosy at night. Wrapped up in this cloak are all our messages of gratitude received and given out to others.

Imagine what your imaginary cloak would look like – what colour would it be? What other colours would be included? What type of fabric would you choose? What would be its style? How long would it be – how heavy or light? How big would it be? Shape it up in your mind to be right for you and one that you would love to wrap around you.

What would you like to weave into it?

There could be some gold or silver threads running through the fabric.

Maybe there are some images to fasten to it?

How would it provide for you? What would you like it to do for you?

Build the picture in your mind so you are very clear on your cloak and what it looks and feels like, so you can reach for it at any time and wrap it around you.

It can be powerful to use this as a visualisation and to sense the swish as you wrap it around your body … as you focus on the colour and how it affects you … how the fabric feels …

Imagine sewing into your cloak of gratitude all the great positive things people have said to you, thanked you for and wished for you … and the words you have shared with people who you are grateful for. How magnificent will your cloak be for you? How will it make you feel?

So carry this forward each day and weave more positive moments of gratitude received and given into the fabric of your cloak and make it something that resonates for you.

Write down what your cloak of gratitude looks like – maybe draw a picture of it.

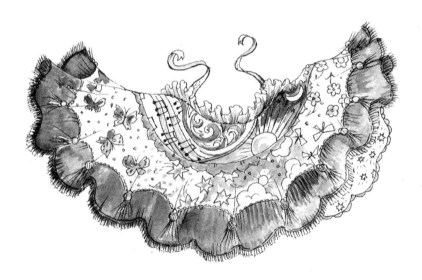

3

Celebrate Each Day with Gratitude

Each new day is special: it is a gift of life and an opportunity to experience life and create a new story on a clean sheet of paper. Consider today what you would like to write on your new sheet and how you can celebrate today in a way that is special for you.

The dew on the grass, the gentle breeze on your skin, the warmth of the sunshine and the birds singing – bringing in a new day. Be thankful.

What would you like to do today that will start to provide for the legacy you wish to leave behind?

What are you grateful for? It could simply be for the air you breathe, the flowers in the garden, the dog that takes you for a walk, the person who smiled at you today, the child that gave you a flower for no reason, the neighbour that popped in to say hello.

Consider all that you have, have had, enjoyed, been blessed with – this thing called life – and smile.

Each day learn how to be thankful for who you know and what you have. Create a flow of grateful energy and this will bring even more to you and surround you with positive thoughts. If you cannot express gratitude for what you have now, how can you bring more towards you in the future?

Expand your thoughts and fill them with the energy of gratitude and sense the happiness within.

A simple '*Thank You*' makes you feel special, doesn't it?

Imagine saying thank you to someone each day for the next month – how special would that be?

Who do you know who would like to hear from you?

Who would you like to send a loving thought and a virtual hug?

Consider sending them a card right now … or picking up the phone.

4

Walking the Road of Gratitude

In the road to your dreams there are many choices to make. As you take a different branch on life's road, take a moment to be grateful for what you have and where you have been: it has shaped who you are and where you are right now.

If we only focus on the things we want, we may forget what we actually already have in our lives. Does that make sense? Being grateful along the way provides the extra energy and drive to nourish your life and who you are as a human being.

I remember meeting a man many years ago when I was training in NLP (Neuro Linguistic Programming) who – from when he was a teenager – knew exactly what he wanted. He admired his uncle, who had created his own business, made great money, and who owned a big house and a top-of-the-range car. So he decided to do the same in his own way. He focused on what he wanted and on his end goal and achieved it all in record time.

'Fantastic,' we may say, and that is what I thought – how wonderful to have such focus and to achieve all his dreams. But as I got to know him, I realised he wasn't happy at all. He had missed the joys of creating and taking pleasure in his business, of his kids growing up and of taking time out for holidays and simply having fun. It had simply passed him by as he'd focused 100% on the goal.

Now I'm not saying this is wrong or right, but I discovered during the time I worked with him that he had only set up this one single goal and – once he had achieved it – he had nothing else set up. So he had lost his way and things around him were not making him happy in the way that, years back, he had expected them to.

By the end of the training he had grasped a new perspective and learned from his journey to date. So had the rest of us – the importance of having the focus and achieving your dreams but of keeping that in balance with living and being true to who you are, being grateful for all you have achieved and taking the time to enjoy life too.

Having a goal is great: living your life and taking time to be who you are, is important too. Take some time out to play and show your gratitude for all you have and all you have achieved; how you have developed and learned over the years; how you have built relationships and friends and how you have taken the time to enjoy the journey.

Take nothing for granted in this thing called life; focus on finding the good in every situation. Be filled with gratitude for what you have, however small, however large – let it nurture your soul and fill you with anticipation of what's still to come along the road.

So what do you take for granted?

How can you switch this around and take just a few minutes to reflect on how grateful you are?

What areas in your life would benefit from some moments of gratitude this week, this month?

5

Messages of Gratitude

I sn't it lovely when you receive a message of gratitude? It warms your heart and makes you feel special, doesn't it?

Sometimes it is so easy to forget the impact of someone calling you or writing to you, to say thank you for a gift or to express their thanks for a piece of work you did or for helping them in some way.

Remember the time and care you took in picking out a certain gift? All the searching for that special something, going from shop to shop or from one online store to another to find that certain colour, style, size or make ... maybe going out into your garden and picking some of your beautiful flowers or baking a cake?

Than perhaps picking up a great-looking wrapping paper and tag and making it look exciting as a gift?

Receiving that big kiss or letter or call of thanks – how did that make you feel?

Imagine if you didn't get a thank you – not such a great feeling!

So, just for today, fill up with all the positive messages of gratitude you can think of. Wrap the positive expressions of thanks into your cloak, as it will keep you warm on dark nights.

Write the messages and thoughts down somewhere safe – create a file on your computer to record them, or put them in your favourite notebook – they will help create a magical feeling again when you need reminding.

When someone takes the trouble to show how grateful they are for something you did or said, accept it – it is a gift for you.

In the moment of the gift of gratitude,

Presented to you in a message

Unwrap it with care and accept it.

Keep it somewhere safe for you

Where the meaning shines so true.

Who can you contact to say 'thank you'?

6

Gratitude Is Here In the Moment

Right now, right here, wherever you are, whoever you are with – be grateful for something. Through taking that moment and being thankful for something in your life, for who you are and what you have, an energy stream will be created for you and others around you.

Live with grace and gratitude and let the energy of the universe feed and nourish you.

It may be you've had a tough week, a tough few weeks. Somewhere amongst all of that, let your mind wander to something that may have happened, however small, that gave you just a second or two of something positive. It could be that someone gave you the gift of their time to listen to you, or that smile someone gave for free as you collected some shopping, or a tune you heard that transported you back to happy times.

Remembering to be grateful for one thing will ease your journey and allow you time to rest when there is chaos all around. Imagine sitting in your very own bubble that's just for you: it fills you with love and energy as you let moments of gratitude weave into your thoughts.

This amazing thing called happiness is within us. It cannot find us or be engineered. It is free for those who spend time being true to themselves, loving themselves and others and with gratitude. We could travel the world to find it and may touch it for an instance in that far-off place. Yet if we return to our home with thankfulness in our hearts and a love of life – it will stay with us.

Feel free to have a moment, just a moment mind, to remember something that meant so much to you – a time when you felt on top of the world, the memory of a warm hand in your hand, a smile that meant something so special to you, a place you loved with all your heart, a friend on the phone, an animal at your side – let it be your moment of gratitude today.

So, maybe this has resonated with you in some way. If it has, then take just a moment now to express gratitude for who you are, what you do, who you know, the gifts you have, the things people have done to help you in some way – whatever works for you. Enjoy that moment.

7

⋆✖⋆

Radio Gratitude

"*Calling everyone*" – *Today is* **Radio Gratitude**. *Put out all your messages of 'thanks' with a smile in your voice – remember all those who helped you over the last week or month.*

"Thank you, John, for the help you gave us on the paperwork … it looks so well organised now."

"So grateful to Jane, for the cakes you baked – they were delicious!"

"Please accept my thanks, auntie, for being there for Bernie – he would have missed his walk without your kind offer."

Please call in and let me have your messages today – who are you grateful for?

Here comes another caller … *"Hello."*

"Hello, I'm calling in to say a huge thank you to my neighbour for picking up our parcel today – so kind of you."

Next caller –

"Today I want to thank my team for all their support with the recent project. We did it – together!"

Remember those who've helped you today

Allow some quiet reflection to be grateful

Decide who to thank directly or indirectly

Inspire others through your example

Open up the possibilities to create Radio Gratitude for yourself

So many more 'thank you' messages have gone out today on Radio Gratitude – the channel for all positive heartfelt messages.

What message would you like to send out?

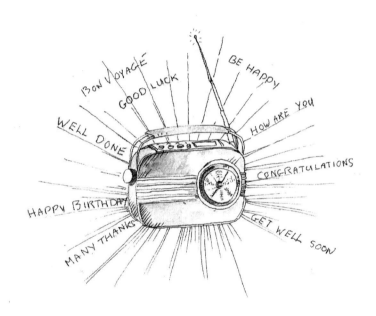

8

🙚

Paint Your Picture of Gratitude

W hat would it look like – your picture of gratitude? Would it contain pictures of your loved ones, your beloved dog, the places you have visited, your holidays, your home, your garden, your dreams, flowers, books, clothes, shoes, bags, jewellery …What colours would you use?

What texture would you choose?

What would be the first thing you would want to paint on your picture of gratitude? And the next? And the next? Capture the sequence for your picture.

This picture could be a mix of photos and painted images and colour to create the sense of what you want to produce and express. It could be completely abstract or completely exact, or shades in between.

How big would it be? What shape would it be?

How would you know when it was complete? Or would it be a picture that you continue to add to?

In the midst of a crazy day, a friend gave me a set of pastels and some canvas. I didn't know what to create but as the day unfolded it seemed like the canvas shouted out to me to capture moments of gratitude and build a picture.

I decided to make a mug of tea and while the kettle was boiling, I thought about what I wanted to include. In a space in my kitchen I put the canvas on the table, opened up the pastels and spread out over the chairs a whole lot of photos I loved.

In the space of only an hour the picture took shape; the people I loved were in the picture – photos and images that expressed my gratitude for them.

Next a few images in pastel of animals and birds I love; an image, even though rather abstract, of the garden. Of other people I was grateful for in my life, some that had touched my life and many that were still in my life. I included lots of other images that depicted things I was thankful for, in a way a series of blessings. Some people may not be able to see all the things I could see in the picture – but each image, colour, picture or word resonated with me.

Some words came into my head and those were added to the picture – I'm sure my art teacher would have told me off for mixing everything up! But it worked for me.

My painting and pictures of gratitude were captured on the canvas. I celebrated and then went off in search of somewhere to put it up.

Let your painting of gratitude come to you in whatever way works for you; let the creation begin and be absorbed in that moment.

9

Who Are You, Gratitude?

I am the thought you have when you are grateful for the sunlight and the moon at night, the birds in flight.

I am the dream you had that materialised into reality and creates a smile on your face each day as you remember.

I am a mystery that some never understood and yet many build into their lives.

I am a token given to others freely, without seeking reward, to warm their hearts and make them feel special.

I am words that express how much I appreciate what you did for me, gave to me.

I am a memory of all the blessings given to me over a lifetime.

I am feelings that resonate as a result of being given the gift of gratitude.

I am an outward-giving force of energy and light in the world.

I am a simple 'thanks'.

I am a smile.

I am laughter and joy.

I am real and yet unreal.

I am loveable and true.

I give and I receive,

I create more and more energy each day.

I am tangible and yet intangible,

I create more, not less.

I grow dreams and memories,

I sing loudly in your heart and other's souls.

I bring peace and love.

I am Gratitude.

10

Miracle of Gratitude

In the midst of a busy day, someone tugged at my elbow and asked for the time. It was a wizened old man with a knobbly walking stick. His eyes were the brightest blue, reminding me suddenly of the sea on a lovely sunny day.

He smiled and it made his white moustache twitch. I looked at my wrist to check my watch and as I did so I realised I was getting late for an appointment, but somehow that didn't seem to matter for that moment. I told him the time and he asked me where Blues Trees, the old people's home, was. I knew it was very near and had a feeling it was only two roads away so I offered to take him there.

He seemed pleased to have my company for a little while and as we walked along he chatted about his life and told me he was visiting the home to see some of his friends there. His name was George but his friends called him Sunny – I could tell why as he was so animated in his stories and so likeable in nature.

He was a kind and gentle soul. We arrived at the home and he was intent on pressing a coin into my hand – it was not necessary for him to give me anything, of course, but he was so keen for me to have it that I gave in. I didn't recognise the coin – it was not one I had seen before – but he told me to take it as a token of his gratitude for giving my time for a while. I told him I had enjoyed my chat with him and thanked him for the gift – which I put in my pocket for safe keeping. I bade him farewell and walked back to get to my appointment.

When I arrived the lady on the desk told me the meeting had been cancelled as they had signed up as a new client with me – without the meeting. I was amazed. I thanked her and decided to go and have a tea in a local café to celebrate.

As I sat down with a steaming cup of tea, I reached into my pocket and pulled out the coin – it was intriguing. As I looked more closely at it, I could see some small writing across it. I could just about read it and it said – *'For those that care deeply for others enough to give freely of time may this bring some magic today.'* It certainly did – thank you, Sunny!

What magic can you bring to someone today?

11

The Spirit of Gratitude

It is in moments of gratitude that our true essence is perceived and in the giving of thanks to someone else is our truth revealed.

The spirit of gratitude can appear

In the midst of a quiet moment

As a fleeting memory

Something that seems unreal

And yet feels real.

Touches your soul

And warms your body

Creates the space

To reach out.

To give thanks

For another day.

It enters invited

Thankful for its coming

Reminders of the blessings

Wrapped in love and light. May today bring you all you need and as you express your gratitude for who you are. May you move towards your dreams and enjoy the moment in the spirit of gratitude.

12

Knocking at the Door of Gratitude

In the middle of the night I woke up with a start and could hear some knocking at my door – or thought I could. There was no way I would answer the door at night so I peered out of the window. The light wasn't on and there was no-one around. I stood and listened again and all was quiet.

I went back to bed and just as I was dropping off the knocking noise started up – what was this all about? All of a sudden I was transported to a place I didn't recognise but one I felt comfortable in. Here I was in a beautiful garden; the smell of the roses was intense and the singing of the birds inspiring. How did I get here and where was it?

I looked down and I was wearing a colourful dress with old-fashioned sandals – goodness, how strange. The sun was shining and it felt warm – rather like a lovely summer's day in the countryside.

As I couldn't see anyone else about, I started to explore the garden. The pathway weaved its way around the various flower borders, taking me on a magical journey of colours and scents. I suddenly realised that the borders were now showing me flowers of all descriptions in each colour – rather like an artist's palette of all the different colours you could imagine. They were blending as one border stopped and another started.

The pathway underfoot was made up of a worn grass path mixed with stones. It kept me on track and moving with anticipation towards the next curve in the garden and the next array of colours.

I still didn't know why I was here, but somehow this didn't seem to matter so much now. I was curious to continue along the path to see what I would find.

Around the next bend in the borders I had a choice to make. Did I take the path towards the purple coloured flowers and trees, or did I turn towards the yellow roses and bushes?

As I peered along both paths, I began to see what looked like an old hut down the purple-lined path – so I decided to take that one in case there was someone around.

The sun was still shining and I began to feel thirsty – hopefully there would be some water in the hut or nearby.

As I arrived in front of the wooden hut, I could see it had a huge door knocker – it looked too big for the size of the hut, and although it was tarnished, I could see a golden tinge to it.

I knocked the door and as I did so it was flung open and a stooped old lady with the most amazing white hair appeared.

"*What is the password?*" she asked. Password! This was more than strange to me – *I didn't know any password.*

She looked me up and down and then smiled and asked me what I liked about the garden – I told her how beautiful it was, how I was enjoying being there and exploring it and how grateful I was to meet someone who could tell me more about it.

Smiling widely, she took my hand and said that I knew the password after all – and I was welcome to come in and have a drink and a chat.

As I stepped into the hut I felt the wind on my hair and a lightness in my body and I was whizzed back to my bed.

Was it all a dream? Yet in the morning by the side of the bed I found a flower – a purple flower – so I took a few moments to express my gratitude for my journey.

I also wondered if I had been outside picking flowers in the night!

The Dance of Gratitude

She swirled her dress and the fineness of the silk rose up and then engulfed the dance floor.

The mix of the robe's bright colours was magnificent and created rainbows in the room and beyond. The ribbons from her hair appeared like shooting stars at night and gleamed beyond the flare, so you could see traces of the energy abound.

The **Dance of Gratitude** had truly begun, radiating the pace and tempo of its power ... so powerful and wondrous in action.

More gratitude was added and the steps increased and with them, a new dance emerged – something so magical, so complete, so breath-taking. The pulse and pace grew, filling up the room with the steps – some small, some magnificent in stride and purpose.

The flow and tempo slowed down eventually as the gratitude stopped coming ... so the dance paused as if to take its breath.

'We need your help' resounded out the message, 'to start the dance again!' **Count your blessings now; put out thoughts of gratitude right now ...** Help restart this Dance of Gratitude. Send all your thoughts of what you are grateful for, send them out and they will be captured by the dance ... Let it swirl and pace; send lots of positive energy out, so we can relax in the knowledge that we are one of many, creating momentum for the world.

Let's dance!

14

Fill up Your Mind with Gratitude

It is better to voice your thanks and your gratitude to someone in the moment or as soon as you can – raise the positive energy today and send out a card to that special someone, send an email, make a phone call, send a text – whatever method you choose, do it today!

Saying 'thank you' creates a positive flow of gratitude within you – it benefits the receiver and the giver. No matter what you believe in, think of things you would like to say 'thank you' for and say it now. Send out a 'thank you' for today, for being alive, for having friends, for having food on the table, for having fresh air to breathe, for having an animal that loves you no matter what, for being able to read a book, write a story, walk to the shop, for having dreams, for having a home, for having someone that cares for you, for simply being you. Raise your energy today – first, as you awake, be thankful for a new day. As you get ready to go to sleep, be thankful for something from the day – however big, however small. Say 'thank you' out loud if you can or whisper to yourself. End the day with being grateful – go to sleep wrapped in positive thought and awake with an aura of happiness and wonder.

Have you ever tried to show your gratitude to people you have met, your friends, your family, people that have impacted your life in a positive way? Well how about taking a 30 Day Challenge and letting all these people know? It's amazing how people come into your mind who would simply love to hear from you. Get into a habit of waking up with gratitude on your mind each morning.

G – Get into a habit of waking up with gratitude on your mind each morning

R – Remember to capture your blessings and note them down

A – Aspire to create more positive moments of gratitude through the day

T – Thank people regularly for the things they do for you or give to you

I – Inspire others to share their moments of gratitude too

T – Think about gratitude and consciously focus on it

U – Understand more about how gratitude impacts on the world

D – Decide to do more, share more, capture more thankful moments

E – Extend your reach of gratitude and celebrate it!

15

Living a Life of Gratitude

Getting up in the morning with gratitude on your mind will create a positive start for you. Feeling grateful for our breath, for being able to reach out and hug someone, speak to someone, hear the birds singing, laugh as your dog or cat dives for the kitchen as they see you walking towards it, see the flowers in your garden – whatever it may be.

By taking just a few minutes each day to reflect on what you do have, rather on what you don't have, will help unlock the energy and create even more for you. Recognise that you are unique: there is no-one else exactly like you.

Someone smiles at you today – smile back.

A friend calls you on the phone for a catch up – say 'thank you'.

Your neighbour pops round with some chocolates for your birthday – be grateful they remembered it.

A bird sits outside your window and sings loudly – listen to its tune.

So many things can pass us by – take a moment to be grateful for all the small things today.

Showing your gratitude each day can change your state into something more productive and positive. By being grateful and showing your gratitude – the world looks more rosy. Living a life of gratitude creates a world full of energy; it can transport you to a positive and wonderful place.

Share your gratitude today – call someone, send a card, do something that will create a smile.

16

Remember Gratitude?

The power of gratitude is in remembering to live it each day. It can act like a beacon of light helping you to find a way into a positive and resourceful state. Being in a thankful mind-set creates so many more possibilities for you. It is rather like beginning to make a tapestry and then realising it is bigger than you thought and with each stitch and colour it glows and expands.

So, on your journey today, keep focused on just one thing you are grateful for and let it fill your being with warmth and love. Let it build an energetic resonance in your day, which shines so brightly that others are drawn to you and want to be with you.

Let a thought creep in of someone special you are grateful for, who has brought into your life something so special that you could sing out loud and be there for them whatever?

And as you travel through your day, be generous with your happiness and gratitude. Give out positive moments to those you meet. Share a smile and a bright "Hello", let the cheer lift them beyond where they are to a higher level.

Be aware of where people are giving you something back too – their gratitude for you and what you have done for or given to them. Be thankful – be sure to let them know you are grateful and say 'thank you'. Never forget a moment of gratitude from someone else; it is a precious moment, so cherish it.

As with every mouthful of the food you eat today, the drinks you drink, or the beauty of the garden so well planted … remember that someone made them happen.

What you give out comes back to you – ever heard of this natural law? So spend time well sending out thoughts of gratitude and giving gratitude to people around you.

Each day there are wonderful things happening around us; it is just the case that we need to notice them. Take some time each day to watch and listen rather than rush and rant. The bustle will still be there but to take a bit of calm and appreciate life is special and creates new energy and drive.

The Gratitude Experience

It is sometimes in those days where nothing seems to be going well and challenges present themselves to us, that we need to take some time out and appreciate what we do have on all levels.

These times can be the very ones that test us and yet they can also be the ones that bring to us a level of gratitude we may never have experienced before. This can be through overcoming challenges and finding ourselves growing stronger. Prosperity comes in many ways and gratitude can help us to understand more about what we already have and through this learning we grow as an individual.

Keep positive thoughts in your head as much as you can. Programming your brain to be aware when unhelpful thoughts pop in can help you to switch to a moment of gratitude, a time when all was well, when laughter reigned and everything was working according to the plan you set up. Counting your blessings, as the saying goes, can be a way to re-align yourself and refocus.

Immerse yourself in the experience of gratitude today: it will fill you up with more energy than you need and will create everything you want. Enjoy it.

The Light of Gratitude Shines Brightly

In the midst of our daily tasks, realising that others are helping us on our way creates a space for gratitude to shine brightly. There are times when we are feeling low – sometimes we really don't know why – and at times through that day we may notice our mood is rather melancholy.

It may be a chance conversation, a letter coming through your letterbox, a card being delivered or a message online that suddenly lifts you back up and re-ignites your spark. The clouds lift and the sun shines again – WOW! It is time then to be grateful and show gratitude for the shift and who helped.

As we become more self-aware, through self-development and through our learning, we grasp the blessings we have received from others. This can then fuel you to give back to others – to show your gratitude each day in any way you can. Get energised and shine brightly for others today.

So how do you recognise your blessings and show gratitude?

How can your thoughts influence your life? It is time to refocus on our thoughts and how we manage them to reflect the power of gratitude now.

T – Think positive thoughts

H – Have a moment each day to be true to who you are

O – Open up to show your gratitude to others

U – Understand more about how to focus on gratitude each day

G – Give out positive vibes

H – Help others to show their gratitude too

T – Take some time to read inspirational books and poems

S – Start each day with a positive thought

19

The Riches of Gratitude

By finding ways each day to incorporate gratitude into your life you create personal riches. You will find yourself happier each day and this will have a ripple effect across other people's lives around you and beyond.

Showing your gratitude and saying 'thank you' to people is so powerful: they are not just words – they radiate an energy and an emotion.

Imagine if everyone showed their energetic gratitude each day to everyone they met … through a smile, a handshake, a letter, a card, a call. What a different place the world would be!

Even if this doesn't happen, each of us can make a difference each day, each week, each month, through little acts of gratitude. Being grateful for what we have and what others have done for us. Like a pebble in a pond, the ripple spreads and impacts on the water as a whole.

Here are some ideas to spread the power!

Send a **thank-you card** – remembering what someone has done for you. Recognise the impact of that action, and how it can make a difference to someone's day.

Give a hug to someone who really needs that comfort – being careful, of course, that it is an appropriate gesture. It is a free gift of love and caring for another human being.

Help someone today – provide that extra support for someone in need.

Meditate on the word 'gratitude' today and explore the meaning.

Give someone a bunch of flowers, a book, a token to cheer them.

Create a daily gratitude ritual – where you write all your blessings in a book and focus on adding to it and reflecting on it.

I am sure you have your own ideas – it would be great for you to share them, to help others and to celebrate your actions.

Gratitude Unlocks Aspects of our Life

Each day the continuation of being grateful for your blessings begins to unlock more in your life. The skills and abilities you once took for granted now become that much more; they seem more important and they take on greater meaning as you can see how you can apply them for the greater good of humanity. Once, what we already have looked small – now it looks more than enough and the expectation for more is not so fixated in our minds. We are grateful for what we do have and share our gratitude.

One weekend, when I was off for a walk in the countryside, at a local park, the car park near the entrance was packed. As I drove round I felt compelled to turn right down one of the small parking areas and saw a woman about to drive out – "Yippee!" I cried. "A space!" I was so grateful to park there and not have to go and park in the nearby field. This was a moment of gratitude for me.

What was your last moment of gratitude? The impact of showing your gratitude each day makes things flow more easily. Perhaps it is simply that recording them on paper or on video, or by sharing them with those you are grateful for, stokes up your energy and focus.

So for today, let's unlock more in our life through showing your gratitude for one thing ... and see what the impact is for you. What's different?

Enjoy!

21

Awake to Gratitude

As you open up your eyes each morning and awake from slumber, think gratitude! Just as your feet touch the carpet or the floor count your blessings and smile – today is a new, refreshed day.

Early in the morning I peer out of my window

The light is lifting and the day is beginning

I listen to the chorus of the birds as they sing

Bringing the new dawn into reality with a zing!

I am filled with gratitude …

It is so wonderful that each day brings a new page for us to fill up – to write a new story on – to meet new people with – to explore new places in. How about for today we maximize our gratitude of wonder at the world and notice the new beginnings from the moment we surface for the day, awake to gratitude, through to the time the night creeps in and the coolness of the evening arrives?

What do you notice?

What things can you write down that you are grateful for?

Sometimes the little things are the ones we miss when we try and count our blessings – we try to think of big things. So, <u>count all of them</u> … capture them … reflect on them … enjoy them.

Consider just for a moment right now – what are you grateful for? What else are you grateful for? And what else are you grateful for?

How about keeping a record for the next seven days of the things you are grateful for? Wouldn't it be a great read at the end of the week? What a wonderful feeling for sure – your own gratitude journal.

22

Gratitude for Happiness

There is something magical about being grateful and showing gratitude for something around you – it creates a spark of happiness in our soul.

This gratitude needs to be expressed outwardly, spoken, written and shared.

How can you do this?

This could be **via a card,** and taking some time to write the words that truly let the other person know why you are grateful for what they did for you. The written word means such a lot to the receiver of the card – it is something they can re-read and keep safely; something they can bring out on a day where they need a boost of positive energy, the energy you sent them! Create some happiness through a simple card today. Perhaps you would prefer to **call them** and speak to that special person? If so grab the phone now – what's stopping you? Speak about your gratitude today. Another way is to **write about** that special person and capture the essence of your gratitude – on your blog post maybe? It is something that can be shared and used to inspire others too. Would you like a great way to write up your thoughts and inspirations?

Whatever way you choose to share your gratitude today, share it! Find a way that works for you and create that extra energy and some happiness.

Gratitude Comes Around

Just like the sun coming up in the morning and the moon shining at night – gratitude arrives in its splendour.

In the majesty of its presence, it's as if it is never forgotten, misplaced or missed.

Like a welcome letter, a memory, a smile, a laugh, a wink, a bird singing, a bell ringing in the distance, the arrival of the feeling of gratitude brings a welcome waft of wind on a hot day. Your breath is precious and takes in a life to be living and a dream to be giving.

Sometimes in the middle of a busy day, taking just a moment to celebrate life restores the soul and gives it the wings to take you forward. Allow gratitude to enter into your thoughts, even if only for a minute or two. Let it give you a hug, a kiss, a memory of something special and engulfing.

Gratitude comes around for each of us – sometimes when we are not ready for it, not really understanding it, yet it arrives and waits for acknowledgement. Be there and let it come into your very being. Welcome it like a friend and give it time to be.

Be a giver too: let gratitude flow from you like a gentle caring stream, refreshing the areas it touches and giving life to those in its path.

Remember the feelings of gratitude each day – never let it slip through your fingertips as if it is not important, because it brings hope, love and freedom to those that listen.

When gratitude comes around to visit, welcome it, nurture it and take it into your life – the sun will shine that much brighter and the moon glisten in its glory. The stars will light the pathway for you as you carry the power of gratitude in your heart and out to others that you meet.

24

Call Me Gratitude

If I were to call your name

Would you answer?

As I walk my path in life would I meet you?

If I took a minute to reflect would you help me?

As I kiss you on the cheek would you feel it?

If I were to sing a song would you hear me?

As I write your name

Would others see you too?

If I were to listen really hard

Would I hear you?

If I talked about you each day

Would it make a difference?

Explore the power of the words, 'I appreciate you', 'Thank you', I am grateful'. As you say these words today, notice how they trigger an emotion. Wrap a positive great moment in a rainbow of colour and love.

It makes a difference to be grateful.

25

The Magic of Christmas – *I am filled with Gratitude*

As a child I would get excited on Christmas Eve – did you? I am filled with gratitude at the memory of this. I would imagine that a burly character with a huge white beard and head of snowy white hair would climb magically down our chimney with a bag of presents.

A mince pie and a drop of sherry was left on the side table to warm him. I used to try my hardest to stay awake so I could hear him arrive, so I could rush out from my bed to see him munching on the mince pie. Alas, I seemed to always fall asleep.

In the morning, once I realised it was Christmas Day I would peer outside my bedroom door and see my red-and-gold stocking bulging with goodies. Here I would find some large nuts (which were lovely), some small sweets, and a few Christmas-wrapped objects.

I would sometimes creep into the lounge to see the tree too, as somehow it always seemed more radiant on Christmas Day.

It must have been early when I would first peer out from my door – I guess parents know what this morning is like, with the kids up even earlier than usual and full of bounce and excitement!

I was lucky: I had wonderful Christmases, ones that still remind me of the feeling of excitement and wonder. To believe and to live the belief of all the stories for many years, fuelled my sense of imagination for years to come.

I am filled with gratitude of these times, as I know many people were not so lucky. In the community where I lived we looked after each other, making sure people were not alone at Christmas and that they had the opportunity for a hot cheery meal and conversation.

In the mist of early youth it seemed like everyone had Christmas – yet in my early working life I came to understand that wasn't the case. Some people were alone, some people didn't even know it was Christmas. Some people were forgotten – so sad. And it's still sad that it can happen today.

So, as we all go about our days coming up to Christmas and through the festive season – give a thought for your neighbours, the elderly people in your street, the young families nearby who are struggling to get by. How can you help? A plate of mince pies, a few seasonal sweets and biscuits, a card, a cake, a few small things wrapped up as a nice surprise from Santa!

Can you be Santa for a day?

Gratitude flows from love – send out some love this Christmas time. Be grateful for what you have – share some gratitude. Send a pretty Christmas card to people you know and people in your neighbourhood – remember others at this time.

Of course this is far wider than just this day – make it a year of gratitude and magic for people around you!

My wish for you is a day filled with magic and wonder and a year ahead of creating the pathway of your dreams.

26

Special Dates of Gratitude

There's a special date in September for two very special people in my life, who got married over 60 years ago. I love listening to their memories of their special day and what they remember, what they saw, how they felt and who shared the day with them.

Memories so precious that they brought a tear to my eye. A love that has lasted, all those years and is still as strong as when they started out on their great adventure.

Seeing a card from the Queen to mark their special day.

This milestone will never be one for me to celebrate and I wonder how many other people will reach this magnificent marker in the future?

So let's think back to remember the special dates we have had in our lives and which dates we may have yet to experience …

- First memory as a child

- First day at school

- First pet

- The first toy of our own

- Christmas Days

- Birthdays

- First party

- First dance

- 18th Birthday

- 21st Birthday

- First day at work

- 50th Birthday

- 60th Birthday

- 70th Birthday

- 80th Birthday

- 90th Birthday

- 100th Birthday and a card from the Queen

- 25th Wedding Anniversary

- 40th Wedding Anniversary

- 50th Wedding Anniversary

- 60th Wedding Anniversary

- Going for your first meal in a restaurant

- Walking in the countryside with that special someone

- Going abroad for the first time

- First Boyfriend / Girlfriend / Friend

- First home

- Favourite author as a child

- Friends at school / at work / at leisure

- Favourite drink / food

- Favourite hobby

- First car / bike

- Wedding day

- Holiday home

- Travelling abroad

- First cruise

- First record you bought

And so the list will build – please add your own special dates to it.

The idea here is to form a list of special memories by remembering different markers and dates in your life.

Record them and allow a sense of gratitude to wash through you and nourish you and create the momentum for more special dates of gratitude in your life in the days ahead.

'And so yesterday brought with it a wealth of memories, some good and some bad, some exciting and some not so exciting – but they have all painted a pattern on my life tapestry. Today I am brightening up the colours and weaving so many more gratitude thoughts into it, so that it will glow long after I am gone. And tomorrow if I am lucky enough to arrive there – I will take time to enjoy life and make the most out of every moment and paint memories clearly and brightly to enhance their glow, and be grateful for them'.

What special dates are you grateful for?

27

🙟

Gratitude – *The Legacy we Leave Behind Us*

There are some experiences that make us think, aren't there?

One such thought is on my mind today – what legacy will I leave behind?

How will people remember me? Will people remember me and what for?

So let me turn this question back to you – what legacy will you leave for others?

Is it one of a loving partner, a loving mother, a loving father, a loving sister, a loving brother, a loving daughter or son, a loving grandmother or grandfather, best friend – whatever the relationship?

Will they remember your kindness, your thoughtfulness, your unconditional friendship, your moments of gratitude towards what they did, your words, your hugs, your letters, the messages you left on Facebook?

Or will they remember what you didn't do, the hurtful things you said, the actions that made them cry?

Be aware of what you do each day; be aware that your words can have an impact on people if they are down, as well as the things you did and the things you didn't do.

Create, from this moment onwards, a legacy you are proud of.

Of course sometimes things happen that we wish didn't – we are human and not perfect!

It is what we do next that matters – make up, say sorry, give a hug, be truthful and be true to yourself.

How do you wish to be remembered?

Build a lasting memory with what you do and say and think. Create an essence around you of gratitude and love. Be true to yourself each day. Be who you are and not someone else that you think you ought to be.

Let your light shine brightly out in the world – so others get drawn to you, and want to be with you and learn all about you.

Help others to do the same.

28

Why Do I Love You, Gratitude?

It seemed so simple to write that note to say 'thank you' yet until I made the time it seemed like I had no time! If I hadn't written that note, you wouldn't have called me, you wouldn't have known I cared and you wouldn't have known how important it was to receive that card from you.

So I love you, gratitude – you bring things closer to me and you provide a door into another wonderful world of positive light and thoughts. Without you this world would be a darker place.

Joy enters when someone is thankful – remembers, writes, calls or simply squeezes your hand in appreciation of something you did for them.

It is like a sunny day, with the warmth of the sun and the gentle breeze caressing your skin, letting you know the world is there for you if you just take a step forward into the gratitude way of living.

Miracles happen within the world of gratitude.

Someone contacts you from 'way back when', someone you have been thinking of but had no way of finding them. The excitement of this reconnection is energising in so many ways.

A business suddenly takes off, when it had seemed it was going to remain dormant. A guide appears to help it get going for real this time: all the work and effort was worth it. The universe had been listening to you – something was not quite in place … then it was and you can celebrate.

Sending out thoughts of gratitude to replenish the positivity in the universe each day sparks that connection to something – we cannot even imagine the impact. Like a ripple in a pond it sends out waves beyond the point of entry – you may see the immediate impact but below the surface even more is happening.

Why do I love you, gratitude?

For all you bring, for all you give, for all you touch, for all you share, for all you see, for all you express, for all you connect with, for all you teach, for all you show us on life's journey and for so much more.

So just for today I express my love for you, gratitude, and send out lots and lots of 'thank you's' into the universe, send out lots of love and lots of moments of gratitude for all that I have and all that I have had.

29

Notes of Gratitude

'Thank you so much for the lovely book you sent me recently for my anniversary – it was so inspirational … thank you for the coat you bought me for Christmas – it has wrapped me in warmth all through the winter and when I wear it I think of you … I am so grateful for the photos you sent me of our last holiday together – they took me back there and reminded me of all the fun we had … I am filled with gratitude over the flowers that arrived on my doorstep from your garden – the scent is out of this world – thank you … I did enjoy our game of golf yesterday – thank you … Our meal out last week was such fun and we had such a great catch up – thank you.'

Do any of these resonate with you?

When was the last time you sent a note of gratitude or received one?

Start now and send out a note of gratitude to someone you know – be the first to send one and maybe start a trend!

By putting a little energy into writing a note and sending it to someone – this could be a card, a letter, an email or a text (whatever works for you) – a smile will be created by the recipient of your note.

This creates such positive vibes in the universe and helps people along with their daily lives. Can you remember a time when someone sent you a note of gratitude or thanked you for something you said or did? How did it make you feel? These are gifts from the universe and are things you can cherish.

I am so grateful that these words come to me and are created by some inspirational moments in my life.

For some moments to come to you, just take a moment and breathe – truly breathe in the air around you. Is it cool or warm? How does it feel to fill your lungs? Does it feel light or heavy, relaxing or invigorating? Now – take a pen and paper and jot down a few thoughts as they come into your head. Share some gratitude today – if only with yourself on how grateful you are today.

30

Opening the Door to Gratitude

It was like a door opening and seeing in front of me a sea of smiling faces … a thought of gratitude was simply enough to fuel this whoosh of smiles and laughter. It felt so good and it lifted my spirits to a high level and to a feeling of abundance.

Sometimes all it takes is a whisper of gratitude in someone's ear, a smile to a passing stranger, to see someone's eyes light up after your gift, a text to a friend who you haven't spoken to in a while. So my challenge to you right now, this very minute – who can you contact with thoughts of gratitude and love? Open the door to gratitude this very moment.

Everyone has a special gift that they may or may not be aware of – it could be their warmth and friendliness, their organisational skills that shine through each time they arrange an event or party, the way they communicate that resonates … so many things they may take for granted because they find them easy and natural to do. Take a moment to let them know you appreciate their special gift and how it makes you feel – open up their understanding so they too can be grateful for knowing and for being thanked.

Opening up your life to feelings of gratitude will open the door for even more great gifts and for more understanding of the abundance that flows to you each day. Can you recognise it?

It can be simple things, complex things, big and small things – whatever they are, they are yours to notice and appreciate.

Some days are full of light and others full of darkness. Take the light days and notice every facet about them, what makes them light – the feelings, the surroundings – and find something in them to anchor them to you. This could be something you can visualise in your mind such as a colour, a song, a rhyme or some item you can hold – as simple as a charm on your keyring.

This will be your lightener on the darker days to lift your spirits and to know without doubt that the lighter days will return to you.

Gratitude can be the bridge across which you reach another place in your heart. This is a place where you feel special and loved. Reach for it each day and nourish the feelings it creates for you. Be grateful for all that you have and have had and will have.

Opening the door to gratitude will bring so many wonderful and amazing things into your life – open up today and be aware of all you have, so that tomorrow will bring even more awareness into your life.

31

Joy of Gratitude

There is so much to do each day – phone calls, meetings, housework, shopping, writing, emails, reading, running around like a crazy person trying to get everything done – that it's time to come up for air! And breathe!

There are people I want to thank today, to show my gratitude to – so taking some time out to do so is really urgent. Leaving it until tomorrow means it may not happen and today is the present for them.

It is so easy when you are wrapped in the busy bubble of life to keep your head down and not come up for a breather. Food and water can be seen to take second place as the day rushes by – nourishment is essential too, so we can flourish and grow in strength to help us manage our lives.

Taking out a small piece of a day to reflect on what we are grateful for, to express our gratitude, can transform our day into something magical and special in an instant.

The routine of daily grind can change to something way above that, something we are suddenly grateful for, as it propels us forward in our personal journey through learning and experience.

What was ordinary grows into something wonderful and exciting, the opportunities we didn't see become visible and our gratitude can bloom again, as we capture those moments in our lives.

Gratitude is so powerful: it can seem elusive until you grasp it again and ask yourself – 'what am I grateful for today?' Take these gratitude moments and make the most of them – wrap them around yourself, enjoy them, share them, write them down, carry them forward and play them again and again.

Thank you for being here today – I hope it provides a moment of gratitude for you.

32

Gratitude is the Secret!

I listened to an amazing webinar all about personal development and goal setting: it reminded me of the keys that unlock abundance – gratitude.

When you set your goals and plant them firmly in your psyche, it is then important that you show gratitude for the progress you make each day towards your goals. However small or large your strides, they are progress. If you slip and slide on a day, just pick yourself up and get focused again. If your goal is strong enough, compelling enough, it will pull you through.

Show gratitude each day for the things you have, the people you meet, the places you visit, anything along the day's pathway that is a gift. Gratitude is such a powerful activity – it increases your energy through doing it and sharing it. And the more you send out, the more the universe will send back in such amazing ways.

Sometimes expressing gratitude may seem like the last thing you feel like doing. The day hasn't gone to plan, the dog chewed your shoe, the parcel you have been waiting for hasn't arrived, the dinner was burnt, you misplaced your favourite book, the local shop had shut early for some reason ... **Time to re-tune** right then! Stop the pattern, switch channels!

Re-tune your thoughts and energy, step out of the muddle into the peace for a moment – it makes a difference. Reset your course for the day or evening – be grateful you can – and celebrate the fact that you changed the course of the muddle.

How can you retune? Put your favourite music on, go for a short brisk walk, potter in the garden, make a drink, call up a great friend, take action to shift your energy quickly.

Find the things that made a difference to you today, the words that triggered a happy thought, the small shifts that helped you. Practise gratitude each day, in whatever way you can. Exercise your gratitude muscle on a regular basis and it will become a great habit that nourishes you.

Over the next few months, through practising gratitude each day and focusing on your goals, the world around you will change and you will have set in motion the journey of a lifetime.

What are you grateful for?

33

Gratitude for Living

After watching a short video, where they were talking about gratitude and how your thoughts can influence your life, I thought it was time to refocus on our thoughts and how we manage them.

Nurturing positive thinking has such power – showing gratitude and being grateful each day allows our true self to shine out and provide that lustre that is infectious for others around us.

So take some time today to tune into your inner guidance: it is there. We need to use it, listen to it and notice it – sometimes amidst the rushing around of day-to-day living, we forget to.

Within your intuition there is true guidance, a wisdom we all have inside ourselves. To build this up, just practise a little each day – be grateful for all the little things. Showing your gratitude for what others provide for you helps create that positive vibe. Take it step by step, as with anything – build it up over time.

Take a walk of gratitude each day. Wherever you may need to go – the grocery store, the local paper shop, to collect your kids from school – and in those walking moments recognise the great things you have experienced in your life, the things you have, the people you know.

Acknowledge yourself too – you are unique and have so much to offer others. Lead by example – show your gratitude, so others can learn this from you.

When you wake up, ensure you bring in positive thoughts. Focus on something that is wonderful – just for that moment – before you get on with your day.

Let's live with gratitude in our hearts and in our minds, bringing in positive moments each day to help make our life absolutely amazing!

34

Gratitude – *Be Thankful Today*

As if out of nowhere, a ray of light flickers on the wall and the promise of daylight arrives as promised! Let's be grateful once again we have light – this is something we tend to take for granted, yet it is so important to us each day to find our way about.

Gratitude can be so easily forgotten in the routine of life and yet if we pause, if only for a second or two, we can express gratitude for those around us, for things we have and hold, for the wonders of the world around us.

I found this poem: I don't know who wrote it, but the essence is clear to read. Enjoy.

Be Thankful

Be thankful that you don't already have everything you desire,
If you did, what would there be to look forward to?

Be thankful when you don't know something
For it gives you the opportunity to learn.

Be thankful for the difficult times.
During those times you grow.

Be thankful for your limitations
Because they give you opportunities for improvement.

Be thankful for each new challenge
Because it will build your strength and character.

Be thankful for your mistakes
They will teach you valuable lessons.

Be thankful when you're tired and weary
Because it means you've made a difference.

It is easy to be thankful for the good things.
A life of rich fulfillment comes to those who are
also thankful for the setbacks.

GRATITUDE can turn a negative into a positive.
Find a way to be thankful for your troubles
and they can become your blessings.

(*Author Unknown*)

So today, amongst all the busy-ness – in what way can you show your gratitude today?

Be thankful for who you are and the gifts that make you, you.

Be thankful for all the lessons you have learnt, even if some of them were hard – they have shaped you.

Be thankful for the people you have met and be excited for people you have yet to meet.

Be thankful for the opportunities that are coming towards you that haven't reached you yet.

Be thankful for the ups and downs in your life as they have taught you about the world.

Be thankful for waking up each morning and having a new day to paint your life.

Be thankful for the small things that make you human.

Be thankful for all your hard days as learning from these can become your blessings in the future.

And, maybe, a moment of quiet reflection to count your blessings …

35

Cultivate Gratitude

Inside the mystery of what makes gratitude so special, there is an effect. This effect is amazing in so many ways – it creates a stream of warmth, of miracles, of ease, of positive happenings, where things just 'turn up'. These things can be totally unexpected and as they happen you suddenly feel special and blessed.

Feeling special and blessed is something you want to nurture and enjoy.

Enjoy these moments and look to create more and more; fit them into your day and into your life with a passion. This passion will grow and flourish and you may notice when you pause that you have a calmness come over you and you feel joy.

In quiet joy, new learning can also grow: as gratitude meanings unfold, they provide you with new clarity and wonder, like the wonder of a child when it first explores the world and marvels at all things around, finding lots of new people, new territories, new toys and many different voices to listen to.

Like the voices of people you love that fill you up with wonderful memories, with words that have meaning to you, that you store in your head and heart, so you can repeat them to yourself when you need them; sounds that resonate with your body and music that plays to your soul.

Your soul is your wisdom – listen to it well; nurture who you are and how you progress in this life in terms of how you live your life day-to-day. Cultivate positivity along the way in all you do each day.

So, as you read these last few words here today – what can you give thanks for right now?

Consider all that you have done and how being grateful now will help you tomorrow to cultivate the habit of gratitude in the days ahead.

Flowers of Gratitude

The garden is full of pretty flowers. The beautiful peonies have opened up their white petals to reveal the most beautiful scent. There are many buds still to come out, which is delightful. Every time I walk past them I bend down to drink in the scent.

The roses are worshipping the sun too as they burst into bloom and reveal their pretty coloured petals to the garden.

Flowers can transport you to a remembered place, a treasured memory and provide a scented hug from the garden.

I am so grateful for the beauty and pleasure flowers bring to the garden and to the home all through the year.

Giving and receiving flowers as a gift is so special, because they light up the home and the garden as they share their beauty with you.

Poems of Gratitude

Gratitude for the Journey of Life

I would like you to imagine

That today is the beginning

Of a new journey in your life.

Let that childlike curiosity

Rise inside of you

And find the wings of flight

To explore and expand

Thoughts and ideas

Emotions and all that is true for you.

Today we begin our journey together

Yesterday was the plan, the concept

Today it is here and begins

To unfold for each of us in our

Own special and unique way.

I would like you to imagine

That you are here in this moment

And that for this moment

Time stands still.

Open up your mind and being

To new learning and experiences

Some things may be familiar to you

Where they are, challenge yourself

And explore the breadth of the opportunity

To become more than yesterday.

Those things that are new

Let them enter in like an invited guest

Who you will entertain and host for

A while – and as the evening comes

Allow those conversations to inspire

And nurture you towards a new tomorrow.

Our journey begins with the intent

To travel, grasp your intent, your

Passion, your desire to be all and

More than you are today.

Drive your passion into adapt-ability,

Response-ability, sense-ability and

Allow the child inside yourself to play

With the ideas you create today

To weave into tomorrow and expand

Into the future, so you can be who you

Really are – unique and special.

So let's embark and set our course

And enjoy the gift of today.

Gratitude for New Beginnings

Today is a beginning of a new tomorrow

If you choose to play the game called life.

Together we can learn about new and different things

To focus on ourselves and others, taking time to reflect.

Into being not just doing, considering how to step up

Should we choose to challenge the status quo,

What we already know, a thought, an inspiration,

A word, a conversation, a feeling, creating emotion.

Let's together begin to dream of all we can and must move into,

Of clarity of our capabilities and knowledge of our power of ability.

To step into a new network with others like us;

Hesitant, excited, anticipating …

Finding ways to support, encourage, so that we can grow together.

Our network becoming infinite ….

A place to come to, feel safe, to explore, learn and grow.

So that as a spark ignited, our full flames can dance

And create the heat and strength to be who we really are

And who we really want to be.

Today is just the beginning …

Intention for Gratitude

Live today with intention

Feel the presence of the present

Feel the joy of being here right now

And the wellness of its intensity.

Be in the present as it brings wealth

Beyond your wildest dreams

Through thoughts and actions

Intensified by your true essence.

Be in the moment NOW

Trust in what you cannot see

Believe all things are possible

And your reality will be so.

Live today with intention

Be true to yourself and your dreams

Trust in the universe and the stars

They will bring you light and love

Walk with a lightness of step

Feel the gentle breeze on your cheek

Touch the flower and sense its spirit

Smile and let the world smile back at you

Just for today, live with intention

Let your dreams unravel

Ask for what you want not need

Let your wishes float to heaven

Allow the time for all to come to you

Believe it is on its way

Be grateful for all your many gifts

Trust in the universal-love array.

Be true, be happy, be focused

For today brings great joy to you

Hugging you, holding you, loving you

Entrusting you with secrets and magic

Just for today

Live with intention

Be who you are

Be free.

Be grateful.

38

Gratitude for Moments of Solitude

When the world is quiet, the dogs are sleeping and the noise of the day is put to bed, moments of solitude are there for the taking.

Sometimes amidst a hectic life, a few moments to reflect and relax can be welcomed.

Take the space to just sit and let the mind unravel the day without you having to order the thoughts or find a solution for something.

Focus on your breathing as it flows in and out helps to calm you and centre you at the end of a busy day.

Final Thoughts

With the bags of gratitude now shared, there is an opening for more circles of grateful thoughts to emerge. I drop into a restful sleep and find myself back in the store full of brightly coloured, many-shaped bags.

There are now more stars flying out of the bags and the ones that were rather dim have now changed and are glowing in the light of grateful thoughts and feelings.

I sense some chattering in the room and the chorus of some song I think I know but cannot name. It feels good to be back here again, an invited guest this time.

'You have fulfilled the dream we all had – now others can be aware of this place and the power of gratitude in the world'.

'Thank you'.

The words are clear and they resonate around the room.

So many others have heard this too, I'm sure, and are aware of the power of gratitude. There are so many ways to be part of gratitude each day.

I wish you a life full of gratitude and one full of magical moments.

With love.

TRICORN
BOOKS